EARNED *Not* GIVEN

WOMEN'S EXPERIENCES WITHIN THE MOTORCYCLE COMMUNITY

S L WALKER, PH.D.
AND SIX ACCOMPLISHED CO-AUTHORS

Published by: SHERO Publishing
getpublished@sheropublishing.com
SHEROPUBLISHING.COM

Table of Contents

Acknowledgment

This book is dedicated to my family and friends who have stood beside me time and time again. They remain committed and on board with everything I have set out to achieve. I am grateful to have family and friends that keep me grounded and humble. Alicia Hinds-Ward, I am speechless. You are truly a blessing that I do not take for granted.

To the strong independent women of SHERO Publishing; Erica Perry Green, Kimberly Perry Sanderlin, and Camilla Moore, I thank you for trusting in my vision and not giving up on me. The coaching sessions and step-by-step guidance throughout the project are second to none. I cannot wait to collaborate with the dramatic trio again.

To the members of Queens of Sheba Motorcycle Club, you never know what directions I am going to lead you. While uncertain at times, you continue to hold on and lean in with me into the turns. In this ever-changing motorcycle community, we were told that we would not last, but we have only just begun. Several have significantly underestimated us, but we remain classy, resilient, professional, and respectful. I thank you for allowing me to lead you. I cherish the Queendom, your commitment, love, and support.

To my soul sister, Traci Renee Braxton-Surratt, you truly understood me. I will always treasure our talks. We shared so much in common. You may be gone, but you will never be forgotten. My Friend, *SiStar*, Queen, and Fellow Aries, may you rest in peace.

To my fellow co-authors and the many known and unknown true lady riders, continue pounding the roads. Riding a motorcycle is not meant for everyone, but clearly, it is meant for you. You are doing the damn thing. I commend you for entering into a community that does not easily accept women. But you did, and you are still here. Some of us ride more and better than our counterparts. Thank you for coming on this journey with me. Thank you for sharing your experiences with the world. I appreciate that you committed to allowing yourself to be vulnerable. Your partnership is an invaluable experience that I will savor for life. I kneel and tip my crown to you. I hold you in the highest esteem. In your willingness to step out on faith and take a risk, you do not have to prove anything to anyone. You proved what the power of women can do when we come together. You earned every blessing that is to come your way. Never let anyone keep you from telling your truth. Certainly, do not let anyone or anything prevent you from getting your dose of *Wind Therapy.*

Introduction

The vision for this book was a long-overdue untold story. Many from afar have seen my challenges within the motorcycle community, but they can only assume. I told a few selected friends who I believe I can trust. Several of them encouraged me to tell my story, to stop disrespectful people from trying to deflate my character by presenting their distorted one-sided views. For a long time, I chose not to speak on the matter. It was not worth the time. I am a believer in God. I know that what happens in the dark comes out in the light. Now, after a decade of repeated challenges and my kindness being taken for granted, it is time to stop the assaults and heal. One way to shut people up is to tell the truth.

Although I was determined to write my story, I knew there were other fellow lady riders who had the same or similar experiences. I wanted to share with other lady riders the opportunity to write about their love and experiences of riding. One story is good, but several stories will surely aid, educate, and hopefully inspire other women to ride.

The whole intent of this book is to help others. This book will help tell stories from club members, independents, and experienced female riders' points of view. The stories will tell how women overcome the challenges of a balanced life, judgment, and injuries and still crave the relief that only comes from *wind therapy*. Whether male or female, the readers will be transported into each co-author's experience of betrayal, pain, fear, challenge, healing, goal-setting, determination, fortitude, healing, and enjoyment. But most of all, *their story, their truth.*

Author Alma Thomas

Author Alma Thomas

Ms. Alma Thomas's professional career is working as an Engineer. She holds a Bachelor of Science in Electrical Engineering from Howard University and a Master's of Science in Computer Information Systems from the University of Phoenix. In addition, she completed post-graduate courses in Management and Organizational Leadership, at the University of Phoenix.

She resides in Southern Maryland, outside of Washington D.C. between the Chesapeake Bay and the Patuxent River, near her immediate family.

She has presented workshops on Information Technology at national training conferences and is a member of several professional organizations. She likes to read, listen to music and ride her Harley Davidson motorcycle.

You Too Can Dream!

On a warm summer day, I sat on the porch watching the traffic on the two-way highway. I remembered that as a middle-schooler I used to dream of owning a car. I would say, "that's my car" when a nice shiny car went past the front of the house. You see, I was a child full of dreams. I loved to read books back then, and my mom used to get books in the mail from a book club for me to read. Reading books taught me to have a vision and to have a dream. I lived in a rural area of Southern Maryland, so those books allowed me to be taken away in the story.

One day some motorcycles came by and my mind traveled beyond the cars. On that day I dreamed of riding a motorcycle. I thought, "I'm going to ride a motorcycle one day!" On another day the motorcycles stopped on the side of the highway and I could see two ladies in the group who were riding their own motorcycles. That confirmed my dream of riding my own motorcycle one day. Then I knew that girls ride motorcycles, too!

Inspiration

It was one of those ladies who inspired me to ride a motorcycle. I met her one day and was impressed. I continued to watch her ride. I would get on the back of motorcycles of male riders, family, and friends. I would watch this lady skillfully riding her own motorcycle in the group of mainly men riding their own motorcycles. I felt so cool to be in her presence. I knew the view from the back was not my destiny. I knew I would be driving my own motorcycle one day. I was paying attention and learning at the age of sixteen and seventeen.

When I turned eighteen, I registered for the Motorcycle Safety Class offered at a local community college. That was a great class because it covered safe driving, hand signals, and all of the things a beginner rider needed to know to be a safe rider. The course included time on the driving range with a motorcycle which was provided for the class. I learned to do a figure 8 and a quick stop using all four controls on the motorcycle without putting my feet down until the bike stopped completely. On the last day of the class, I completed the written and driving skills test. I received the certificate of completion and I was able to take that certificate to the motor vehicle administration to get that Class M license. I still practice those driving skills today on twos (motorcycle) and on fours (cars).

As years went by and after I had completed my college degree, that lady rider I saw as a little girl was now family through marriage to one of my family members. I continued to admire her motorcycle journey as a member of an all-female motorcycle club. I participated in many of the fundraisers of that club, which were straight-out cabarets to party and have a good time. I admired the motorcycle clubs for performing many acts of service to the community. Services to the community included food drives, coat drives, scholarship fundraisers, escorting funerals and more. I admired the stories of the road trips and I still dreamed of the day I would have my own motorcycle to ride.

Mentoring

At that time, I was admiring that lady rider in her woman-hood journey as well. She became a mom to her own child. She was like a mentor and she was teaching me how to maneuver in sisterhoods inside and outside of the motorcycle community. I was also watching her journey as a Christian, which you should already know is continuous and never complete.

I still yearned to ride my own motorcycle. Heck! I was already driving a five-speed car and I loved the speed. Speed was in my system. When I decided to purchase my own motorcycle, I consulted with a few people. Questions were…should I get a small bike? What color should I get my bike? Should I get a Harley Davidson Street Glide? She said, "Get what you are going to ride and learn to ride it". A male rider said, "Get any color you want because you are paying for it".

My friend and mentor would call me on Sundays, after church saying," After I cook dinner for my family, we are going out so you can practice riding for a while". She would pull up and say, "Where is your lipstick and earrings, you are still a girl?" Then, she would say okay, "Let's pray before we get on the motorcycles". That is when I started feeling the importance of women holding their position in the motorcycle community. We would turn heads when we rode; people would point and look across the highway as if to say, "Those are girls riding those motorcycles!" We would ride until dark. That is when I learned the importance of having tinted goggles for the day and packing clear goggles to change into for the ride home after dark. There were not as many lady riders back then as there are now. We were earning every woman's position in the motorcycle community.

The Fun of the Experience Rider

I joined a Harley Davidson Only Club that was close to the town where I currently live. That was a way to be sure I would always have someone to leave town and to return to town with when we did road trips. The club had been all-male riders. Once I was in the club, they trained me to ride in a group formation. They taught me how to keep proper distance between bikes when group riding. The rule was no lagging behind and to hold your speed in the group. When one of our members would call out "Turn Up", I knew that meant open the throttle and hit 100 miles per hour! It felt scary at first. After several trips with my club to North Carolina, South Carolina, Philadelphia, and Ocean City, I would ride in the second position and I would tell the leader of the group to "Turn Up". One thing was for sure, you had to ride your own twos. No one could do it for you.

I always wore a long braid down the back of my head and lipstick, and earrings, so people rolling up on my club from the back would know that I was a girl. Other clubs would sometimes roll past us and nod at me because I was the only girl in the group riding the highway from state to state, to week-long bike gatherings in other states.

My mentor told me to avoid the conflicts between the motorcycle clubs and to treat other ladies with respect. Mind your own business! She said, "I have seen women get caught up in the community, but don't let that be you". She said, "Keep the girl code. Make friends and respect the other ladies in the community". She always wanted to help another lady learn how to ride. She laughed and spoke to everyone in the motorcycle community. If you were with her, you were going to have fun and meet new people because she was a people magnet.

I made and renewed lifelong friendships. I met preachers, lawyers, doctors, police officers, plumbers, homebuilders, nurses, hairstylists, engineers, and a lot of other professionals riding their own twos. I met golfers, runners, chefs, card players, racers, and a lot of other hobbyists within the community with whom I shared similar interests. If you didn't know a person personally at an event, but the two of you knew another rider, that made you cool, and you were in the circle. Motorcycle riding became more than just freedom and *wind in my hair*, it became a part of my identity. People that never knew my birth name would speak to me by my club name.

The Rainy Ride to Rockingham North Carolina

As I gained more skills as a rider, I felt comfortable taking out-of-state road trips. We had ridden to Rockingham, North Carolina before without incident. When we started this trip we did not know how different it was going to be. As we rolled past Richmond, Virginia the rain showers started and we continued to ride. We didn't have on rain gear. Keep in mind that Harley Riders roll down the road from tank to tank. Those 200 miles or more can be a lengthy ride.

As we continued in the rain, we had the family and wives of some of the riders following us in cars. We could barely see the highway as we entered North Carolina. I was not riding second position that day because I would have suggested that we stopped somewhere to get cover. We finally made a gas stop and everyone was soaked through and through for riding almost 2 hours in pouring down rain. My braid was dripping water. It was at that stop that the people traveling behind us in the cars said that other cars would pass them and almost cut in on us because they could not see us in the rain.

After getting gas we continued on the way to Rockingham and almost made it to the hotel. At this point, one more shower wouldn't make a difference, so it started raining again! Once at the hotel, some of the guys went out to purchase sneakers to ride in, because they said their boots were too wet to ride in for the next couple of days.

The Gospel Ride to Philadelphia, Pennsylvania

I met up with a church group including the preacher to ride to Philadelphia, Pennsylvania. The ride plan was to meet up with another affiliate club of the same Gospel riders that was based out of Pennsylvania. I knew this would be a safe cruising ride. A lot of the members were older males, some with females on the back. I didn't know who the pastor was on the ride, and it didn't matter. He was just another Harley Rider that day in the eyes of bikers. We rode across the Chesapeake Bay Bridge in Maryland and through a small town in Pennsylvania. As we passed over small brick crosswalks in this two-lane town, people looked as if they were not expecting eight Harley Davidsons to be rolling through their small town. I guessed the leader's GPS routed us right into the middle of this small town. All the loud pipes on the Harleys turned the heads of the people strolling the streets and those in the cars.

The Long Ride to Desoto Texas

We met at 5 am to get on the road to ride to Texas. I had a car come by to get my luggage and take it to the meeting location to be put in the trailer. One of the members was driving a truck and pulling a trailer for the trip. It was a good idea to have access to a trailer on a 1350-mile trip just in case a rider experienced an illness or a bike broke down. The spirit is- no rider gets left behind!

We rode from Maryland into Virginia and, on a gas stop, I was getting sleepy. Yes, you can get sleepy on a motorcycle. One of my club members convinced me to get a B-Energy shot. Well, it kept me awake. This was the longest trip for me with the club; riding to Texas by way of an overnight stay in Tennessee. When the club made it to Tennessee, people from our hometown were celebrating us on Facebook. The hometown was claiming bragging rights for our hometown club

On the second day we pulled out of Nashville and headed for Memphis. After a quick bite to eat in Memphis we rolled on past the St Jude's Hospital and on to Arkansas. That was the trip when my club passed by Shorty Rock and her club. I remember seeing the two ladies riding in her group as I followed the tradition of my club of rolling down the road. The code was we roll 10 to 15 miles above the speed limit most of the time.

The ride into Texas during the month of July was extremely hot. I always said when I saw the stars and state symbols on the overpass as we got closer to Dallas was when I felt like I was a turkey baking in an oven! When we arrived at the hotel after the twelve hours of riding from Nashville Tennessee to Desoto Texas, I was extremely dehydrated and I just wanted cool drinks and air conditioning.

Traits of Lady Rider

As I look back on the character traits that were needed to be able to ride a motorcycle 700 miles in one day to Memphis Tennessee and get back up the next day to ride the remaining 700 miles to Desoto, Texas, I would say number one is **self-confidence.** You need to know in your mind that you have the ability to get it done. The second would be **resilience.** You need to be able to recover quickly from difficulties and to be tough. The third one is to **maintain self-respect.** That is to maintain a sense that you are behaving with dignity. Keep the determination and purpose for doing it with structure. I had the drive to learn and I wanted to be good enough to ride with anyone and along to any place. That was such a sense of accomplishment; based entirely on your own skill and performance.

Carrying the Torch!

I know lady riders that are now in heaven. I continue to pray before I ride and to carry the torch in the spirit of lady riders. I continue to ride in honor of lady riders who may have given up on the sport. I continue to ride for those who may have taken a pause to raise their children or to become caregivers for elderly parents or spouses. I also ride for those yet to learn to ride motorcycles, like the little girl I walked behind while she was riding her bicycle with training wheels. I showed her a picture of my bike on my phone. I asked her, "Do you think you will ride one of these one day?" She said, "Yes." That is the beginning of a dream!

aka Casper

Notes

_____

_____

_____

_____

_____

_____

_____

_____

Author Dawn Phillips

Author Dawn Phillips

Dawn Phillips is an enthusiastic, energetic, compassionate, and health-conscious woman who loves to utilize her creative skills in the form of writing. She recently relocated to Lakewood, Colorado, where she resides with her husband and their dog Savannah. Together they have four adult children (three boys and one girl) and nine beautiful grandchildren (five girls and four boys). Her full-time job is as an Administrative Officer with the Department of Justice, Environmental Natural Resources Division located in Denver, Colorado. She is also the Owner of Dawn's Conscious Living & Lifestyle Coaching where she focuses on helping individuals change their mindsets and behaviors in order to live a happier and healthier life.

Furthering education is important to her; as a result, she is currently completing her bachelor's degree in psychology with a tentative graduation date of Spring of 2024. She is proud of the certifications she has earned as a Mindfulness Meditation Facilitator, Life Coach, Health Coach, and Functional Nutrition Specialist. It is important for her to follow her God-given purpose and is often referred to as an empath.

In February of 2019, she became an author by publishing her first book entitled, *Your Voice Your Choice – Free from Past Pain*; a story of how she persevered through her experiences with domestic violence. Her second published writing was in the form of an interactive workbook, and it is entitled, *Self-Love Is the Best Love – Where Your Journey Begins and Ends Is Up to You*. Both books were birthed out of personal experiences with hopes that she can help someone avoid some of the same mistakes she made and eliminate some of the fears, self-doubt, insecurities, and hurt that she endured for decades.

Dawn realized she had a love for riding motorcycles at a very early age, and in 2010 she took the riding course, obtained her endorsement and purchased her first motorcycle. Currently, she enjoys riding her 2018 Road Glide Special and often refers to riding as therapeutic. Among the list of her many riding accomplishments, there are four cross country rides, completion of rides to 48 states plus Canada and Mexico, and rides to two of the four corners of the U.S. She has also achieved multiple ground pounder awards and numerous iron butt challenge completions. She serves as a mentor for new riders and has had the privilege of taking a few ladies under her wings. Dawn is looking forward to the next chapter in her life - retirement in the summer of 2026 and spending more time traveling, riding her motorcycle, and being with her grandchildren.

Website: www.coachingwithdawn.com
Facebook: Dawn UnapologeticallyMe Phillips
Email: DawnPhillips@dawnscllcoaching.com

I Just Wanna Ride!

I knew from the time I was a toddler that I wanted to ride a motorcycle. I vividly remember riding on the back of my dad's motorcycle. My mom tied me around his back with a rope because my arms could not reach around his stomach. She feared I would fall off if I was not secured properly. Another moment that stands out is when I was in elementary school. My dad was taking turns riding the kids in the neighborhood around the block. When it came to my turn, he took me out of the neighborhood and down the road we went. To this day, I remember the feeling of excitement being on a motorcycle and the sense of freedom that resulted from those rides.

It wasn't until I was in high school and started dating that I was afforded the opportunity to ride on the back of a motorcycle again. I dated two guys that owned motorcycles. My dad, despite being a rider himself, opposed me riding on the back of anyone's motorcycle and went as far as forbidding me from doing so. I didn't see anything wrong with it and defied his wishes. One warm summer day, I had been out and about with friends with plans to ride with my boyfriend later that afternoon. It happened to be my younger brother's birthday and I knew our family would be celebrating later that evening. My boyfriend would have to pick me up down the street so my dad would not hear the roaring pipes. I anxiously awaited the feeling of the wind on my face and my knees in the breeze. We rode mostly back roads, and he was careful not to go too fast knowing he had precious cargo on the back. When we stopped for gas, I was in the process of dismounting the bike when my leg pressed against the hot pipe. I suffered a severe burn and was in quite a lot of pain. The only thing I could think of at that time was "my dad is going to kill me". There was no way I was going to be able to hide my injury. Let's just say it didn't end well and I wound up being punished for two weeks.

As I got older, the men I chose to marry did not ride. That was never an issue for me. I had my first child when I was twenty and my last child when I was twenty-six. My focus was on my children and riding a motorcycle was the furthest thing from my mind. I could not fathom the thought of putting my wants and needs before theirs. Riding is an expensive, time-consuming hobby and there is the obvious - it can be dangerous. My children deserved to have my undivided attention without having to fear I may not come home. I did not make the decision to ride until my youngest child was 14 years old. I felt she was old enough and all three of them were self-sufficient. They required less of my attention, so I started looking into purchasing my own motorcycle.

When I turned forty, that seemed to be a significant time in my life. I wanted change. I wanted more. I had lived over half of my life taking care of everyone else. I denied myself things that I wanted because it was the right thing to do. My husband at the time did not approve of my wanting to ride. He thought I wanted to do it as a way of meeting other men. Little did he know, the only thing on my mind was to recapture that feeling of having the wind blowing in my face and the sense of freedom that came along with it. My decision and determination to ride was the icing on the cake and the straw that broke our marriage up.

I wasn't sure where to begin on this new journey and ended up turning to social media. A friend of mine from high school rode and I would always see him post pictures of his motorcycle. I soon realized he was the President of a local MC. It wasn't long before he invited me to come and attend one of their club meetings. I agreed and at first appearance, they seemed to be a great group of individuals. They welcomed me with open arms and portrayed themselves as family. I was elated and very naive. Before I knew it, I had become a member and had not gone through any period of prospecting. To be honest, I had no idea what it was to prospect nor was I knowledgeable about protocol. I was just happy to have found a group of individuals who appeared to love to ride as much as I did. They helped me pick out my first motorcycle and even drove me to North Carolina to pick it up. Because I had not gone through the riding course yet, I was not able to ride right away. They let me keep it in their storage unit in the meantime. Shortly after, I took the course and passed. I was officially endorsed as a motorcycle rider.

In the beginning, it was great. I was appointed the Secretary of the club and was fitting in quite nicely with the other members. We rode locally as a club and attended events. What I didn't know is that there was some very shady activity going on behind the scenes and behind my back. This is the part that I don't like to talk about and most people don't know. I started having people come up to me and ask me if I swung both ways. I couldn't understand why until it was brought to my attention that the President, my supposed friend, had been going around telling others that I was involved in a threesome with him and his girlfriend. In addition, he was secretly trying to set me up with men, some of whom were married. At that time, I wasn't aware of the stereotype that all women bikers were easy. I was being taken as a joke and there were men out there who thought I was just another chick who was ready and willing to give up the goods. Right around that same time, I received a call from one of the other local club presidents. He wanted to meet me for lunch and had something important to share with me. When we met, he informed me that I should consider leaving that club as he feared my safety. What he told me next shook me. The President of my club had been dabbling in some activity with one of the local outlaw clubs and not in a good way. He was putting himself in harm's way with no regard for his members. My being new to the scene did not help because I didn't know much about outlaw clubs or what they were capable of doing. I took heed to the warning and advice and decided that was not something I wanted to be involved in. Shortly after, I turned in my colors. My leaving the club so abruptly was not well received and as a result, led to almost a year of constant harassment by my ex-President. He had random women harass me. He would threaten to be waiting for me when I got home. He often made mention that I needed to watch my back which caused me to become extremely paranoid and fearful every time I left my home. It got so bad that I ended up filing a restraining order against him. All of this made my first experience with an MC almost unbearable.

Once that traumatic experience was behind me, I was fortunate enough to link up with some members of a local riding club. Again, they were very nice to me and willing to work with me to get my skills up. I was considered a "hang around" for a while. I thought it was a good fit, so I decided to become a member of that club. Before I knew it, I was voted in as their secretary. This was a slightly different experience for me since they were sanctioned as a "riding club" and were not governed by the same protocols as an MC. It was my understanding that they received their required blessing by a local dominant club, and nobody bothered them. In a relatively short amount of time, I realized I had made yet another poor decision. They were more of a local riding club rather than a long-distance riding club and this was stifling me from expanding my riding by crossing state lines. I felt very restricted. They mostly attended local events such as cookouts, bike nights, annuals. None of them did much distant riding. I wasn't in it for the parties and riding from town to town all within the same state. At one point, I was told that I could not ride alone because it wasn't safe. All I wanted to do was ride and I could not understand why members of a riding club did not encourage and support my desire to ride more, and ride long distances.

This club was co-ed, however, there were only four women who were members including myself. The significant others of the men club members wore vests with patches on them that were the same as mine, but they did not ride. I could not understand how that was allowed and when I asked, I was told that was none of my business. As I began being present a lot more, that is when the whispering and rumors started. Here I was a nice-looking single woman who's only objective was to ride her motorcycle and I found myself being accused of wanting their men. There was a lot of "who does she think she is" and unwarranted jealousy. Why was it that just because I was single, it meant that I was trying to get in everyone's pants? The wives and girlfriends did not speak to me. They didn't even try to get to know me. It got so bad that the Vice President, who happened to be a female, started hating on me simply because I got along so well with her husband who was also a member. I could literally feel the tension when I was in the same room as the other ladies. For a while, I was able to look past their insecurities and focus on my goals, as I was not willing to entertain their foolishness. I found myself gravitating toward the few members who liked to ride outside of the local commuting area. That local riding was simply not enough for me. Myrtle Beach Bike Week came around and one of the members asked if I wanted to ride down with him. I jumped at the opportunity. At the time, I was riding my Kawasaki Ninja 636 and had not ridden further than a couple hundred miles at a time. This was the pivotal point in my riding as that is when I earned a lot of my respect from fellow riders. Others could not believe that I rode my sports bike from Maryland to South Carolina. The attention I had been receiving slowly turned from me being a nice-looking single woman who was out to steal married men to my being a badass woman who loved to pound the pavement while crossing state lines. When I returned from that trip, it wasn't long before I decided that club wasn't for me either. For a second time, I turned in my colors. Now, I was concerned that I would be perceived as a "club hopper". If you are involved in the motorcycle community, you know that you are not taken seriously as a rider if you are constantly jumping from one club to another. I was at risk of tarnishing my reputation; the reputation I worked hard to establish. I had to follow my gut regardless and decided to part ways amicably. Thankfully, the actions of my now ex club members were reciprocated, and I was able to remain friends with many of them even to this day.

I started making acquaintances with more and more fellow riders who genuinely shared the same passion as me which was always for the love of the ride. Some were local while others lived out of state. I began putting myself out there more by attending events; particularly those that involved some type of ride some-where. I was riding out of state to support other female riders when they were holding their events. I've always felt it's important to establish connections when you are a rider for various reasons. You never know when you might need a mechanic, a place to lay your head, a source to tell you the 411 of what is going on in their area, and just someone who will look out for your best interest. In my efforts to step outside of my comfort zone and spread my wings, I met and started dating my now-husband.

My husband was the President of an MC in Ohio which is where he was residing when we began dating. It just so happened a chapter of that MC resided in Maryland, and I was already familiar with a few of their members. I started hanging around them more to get to know them and it wasn't long after that I became a member of that chapter. For the first time, I was introduced to what it was to prospect as well as becoming familiar with bylaws. This chapter was also co-ed and there were only 3 female members outside of myself. One of the ladies sponsored me and we quickly bonded with one another. Despite the initial period of feeling welcome and connected as a family, my third attempt to be a part of a motorcycle club ended in my turning my colors in once again. At that time, I had really begun to blossom as a rider and wanted to have the freedom to ride with whomever I wanted as well as wherever I wanted. When you are a part of an MC, there are rules in place and those rules are made to be followed. You must respect the authority of the club President as well as those who hold a position as one of the officers. My decision to walk away was based on what I thought was in my best interest and was not a negative reflection on that MC. I had decided it was time to become and remain an independent rider. I can honestly say without any reservation that it was one of the best decisions I ever made in relation to my riding.

Being an independent rider played a significant role in the many goals I've been able to accomplish, and I am proud of who I am as a rider. My husband and I completed our 48 states together. A journey we did not start together but finished together. I have led three cross-country rides from Maryland to California and will be doing my first solo cross-country ride in May of 2022. I have ridden in Canada, Mexico, and two of the four corners of the United States. I have completed numerous iron butt challenges and received a few ground pounder awards. I took on the role of being a mentor to new riders and have had the privilege of mentoring a few ladies. It's a truly rewarding experience to take women under your wing and watch them mature as riders. Riding has taught me many lessons such as the importance of always keeping your head on a swivel, staying hydrated, packing properly (less is best), being prepared for all four seasons no matter what the weather forecast is predicting, having a tracker app for both weather and for those who want to follow you on your journey, ensuring your finances are adequate for each trip, carry sufficient insurance, and most importantly…expect the unexpected.

If there is one message I can convey to my fellow lady riders, it would be to stay true to who you are. When you are a member of a club or even simply a part of the motorcycle community, stop trying so hard to be seen. You end up losing yourself in the process. Your riding will speak for itself and that is where you will gain the respect of not only your fellow wind sisters, but of the brothers who ride as well. The more you try to prove yourself by doing all the wrong things, the less you will be taken seriously. There is a phrase that comes to mind "you don't get respect by laying on your back; you get it by riding your bike". Stop being messy and thinking this is a competition. You can do this by staying in your own lane; there is less traffic there. Riding should always be about having fun and enjoying what we love to do. Don't give others a reason to think we do not deserve a place within the motorcycle community.

aka White Chocolate

Notes

_____

_____

_____

_____

_____

_____

_____

_____

Notes

_____

_____

_____

_____

_____

_____

_____

_____

_____

Author Jen Hoag

Author Jen Hoag

Jen Hoag was born in Seoul, South Korea. She was adopted and raised around the world as an Air Force brat. She now resides in San Antonio, Texas with her husband and three fur-babies. She earned her Bachelor's in Psychology from Wichita State University. She then joined the United States Air Force in 1997. She became a Certified Alcohol Drug Abuse Counselor and held many positions at eight different duty locations and her three deployments throughout her 20 years of military service. While on her second deployment, she began her Master's in Forensic Psychology and completed it while stationed overseas. After retiring from the military, she returned to school and earned her Master's in Social Work and is now a Social Work Fellow with the Steven A. Cohen Military Family Clinic at Endeavors in San Antonio.

She enjoys working with veterans and their families. Her focus is on evidence-based therapies for trauma and post-traumatic stress disorder (PTSD), and she is also trained in other various cognitive behavior therapies.

Jen is also a Senegence Consultant for long-lasting makeup and skincare products under the label Jen U Wine Lips. She enjoys making people feel and look good around her.

She and her husband also volunteer with Gizmo through Pets Are Wonderful Support (PAWS) for Service at the local Veteran Administration hospital providing animal therapy. She is also involved in providing food and other necessities to underprivileged individuals in the community through multiple agencies, including the motorcycle club.

At the time of this publication, Jen is still recovering from her motorcycle accident. When she recovers, she will return to riding, volunteering, gardening, drinking wine, and hanging out with her rescue dogs.

Contact information:
Email: jen.hoag73@gmail.com
Email: jenuwinelips@gmail.com
Facebook: JenUWineLips
Instagram: JenUWineLips
https://senesite.senegence.com/jenuwinelips

How I Earned My (Survivor) Patch

How did I get there?

N ow as I reflect on the question, my answer is-
"I survived!" I survived just like I did coming into this
world. I was born as an orphan and survived then, so my legacy is
surviving. And no, my name is not Gloria! I think it is best to go
back to what occurred almost a year ago to understand what I mean.

It was a warm day, just as dawn was breaking. We had just
ridden over 800 miles the day before. We hopped on the bikes, went
to get gas, and started north. It was 45 minutes later when it all
changed. We were going 70 mph and started braking because we
wanted to get to the right lane behind a big rig. I braked to 40 mph
and the brake was holding until I felt my rear tire starting to fishtail. I
tried to align the front tire and then it happened; I felt the bike going
down. Within a minute, I felt my bike slide to the left and forward
on my fairing. I flipped over the bike and slid. I got up and was bent
over like a dog; panting and a bit disoriented. As a rider, we always
talk about when we will go down; it is never an "if." Previously, I
went down in the Dolomites and I was riding by myself at the time. I

did not have an alternate plan. I survived. This was my second time, but the first time, I had picked up my bike and was able to finish the ride – not this time. After being transported to the regional trauma center, they determined I had a laceration on my liver. I was cleaned up and transported to a Trauma 1 Hospital located four hours away. Throughout the ordeal, I was conscious the whole time.

My husband was two bikes behind and saw every-thing. He stayed with me and drove his bike for 4 hours behind the ambulance. During this time, I knew I was being taken care of, so I worried about him. We made a stop midway through the state, so he could gas up and get a little bite to eat and some water. We made it to the hospital and I was in the trauma bay for hours. While I was in there, another patient came in through air evacuation. He had been four-wheeling and flipped his quad over a barbed-wire fence. I compared myself to him. I did not require surgeries or intubation like him. I did not have to be air evacuated like him. I was not bloody like him. I did not have any broken bones like him. I was lucky.

I was finally taken upstairs to the ICU room. The ward said "Cardiac/Surgical ICU." I had no broken bones and I did not lose consciousness. I am lucky. They bandaged me up. The next day I was finally moved to a regular medical ward. I was told I could have regular food. Nothing sounded good. I did not want to go to the bathroom more than I had to because my right cheek of my bum hurt from sitting on it. My husband stayed with me for as long as he could each day. We talked about how we were going to get home, which is normally an 11-hour ride. He left his bike at the local Harley Davidson dealership and rented a minivan. After 4 days, I was discharged from the hospital with a suggestion of some supplies I could use to reapply bandages and a two-day prescription for medication. This is going to be fun!

We went to the hotel that my husband was staying at. I laid in bed and he went to the store to get what we thought we would need; adult diapers, since I needed help sitting on my right cheek and clothes since I was released in a hospital gown. All my clothes had been cut off of me just days before. He also purchased shoes and socks, since I was not going to wear my boots. How was I going to be able to sit in a car for any length of time? I needed a pillow to cushion my seat. Now, we had our supplies and a plan. The next day we left. I had a feeling that I was not going to make it the whole ride back home. Surprisingly, I made it six hours on the first day, not bad! When we left the hotel room, it looked like someone had been murdered there. Blood and bandages overfilled the trash cans as we retreated my wounds and prepared for another day of travel.

We finally made it home the next day. I called my primary care office to request home health assistance to change the bandages and they said it would probably not be activated until the next week. They suggested that I could go to the nearest ER for treatment. The next day, I went to the local ER which was a military ER. I told the nurse what needed to be done. I needed my bandages to be changed. They put me in a room and the doctor came in and told me another doctor would be coming in. Fast forward two hours and the doctor stated that I needed to take a Covid-19 test and I was not going to have my bandages changed. I was going to be admitted to the hospital. What?!? Okay, it probably will be the same as the previous hospital, but since it is a military hospital, maybe they can get me home health assistance.

The nurse came in and said, "We need to clean your wounds." I quickly replied, "Okay, but it will not occur without pain medication." They injected me with pain medication and scrubbed. I was tired, but *I survived.* Sore, but I never lost consciousness. I did not break any bones. The doctors examined me and told me I was going to have surgery on Monday. They informed me that all the areas, which were covered by bandages, were going to require skin grafts. I thought to myself, "Oh, so it's more severe than I thought, but I did not lose consciousness and I did not break a bone." I still had pain on my right side, so the doctor needed to find out why. The doctor informed me, "You will get a CT scan tomorrow."

The next day, they clean the wounds and it was time to get a CT scan. After the scan, I returned to the room and two hours later, the nurse said that I was going down for surgery.

"Wait. You said on Monday?!?" I quickly asked.

"You have a grade 5 laceration on your liver. We need to put a mesh down your jugular to keep the clot from traveling" the physician informed me. Apparently, clots that travel can cause a lot of damage or death. A couple of hours later, I returned to the room with a bandaged slit in my jugular. "At least tomorrow my husband and I can sit and read the paper and relax," I thought to myself.

Sunday evening, we were talking about how the week would look. My husband needed to go to work and he would visit in the afternoons during the visiting hours. It took two hours for the nurses to bathe me and to get me bandaged up again. Then, my husband and I both got a text.

"What is this? What does this mean?" my husband said, "This text says the accident was not your fault! You were rear-ended!" I looked at my husband in disbelief.

"Wait a minute, while I was talking with the police and others from the club were asking me questions, no one spoke up. Are you saying that the person who just texted us, rear- ended me?" My mind was racing. Not only is this man a brother in the club, but he is also a Brother in Arms. No integrity?!? I cannot respond. My heart is pounding and I felt anxious. I had a surgery in the morning and my mind needed to be right for that. I needed to calm myself. Later, I found out the term for what I was is *moral injury: a strong cognitive or emotional response from a transgression.* This occurs more frequently than we acknowledge.

Fast forward a few days, and I responded to the text to see if the person wanted anything and the person said they just wanted to make sure I was "good." I thought to myself, I see clients for *their* issues, of course I am good. I am a survivor. After a month of treatments, my body was not healing as quickly as I wanted it to, but apparently burnt skin does not typically heal in less than a year. I wish I had been told this earlier so that I could have adjusted my expectations for my healing. After finding out mu capabilities for myself, I discovered that I can do most things unless it required me to sit or lie on my right bottom cheek.

I am a person who never had an alternate plan if I have one now. I did not have an alternate plan when I was interacting with other clubs on the set; having to ensure they respected a club officer. I did not have an alternate plan when I was the only female prospecting into the club. *I survived.* I did not have an alternate plan when I decided to go to graduate school during a deployment and two permanent changes of station. I did not have an alternate plan when I was dealing with toxic leadership in Kuwait. *I survived.* When I returned from deployment, I was told by the Safety Official that he did not have to worry because no one in the group looked like a motorcycle rider. I did not have an alternate plan. When I was informed of my grandmother's death, I knew what I had to do. I took the last plane from Turkey to my grandmother's funeral and four generations were waiting for me to arrive since I would have been the only family member not present. I did not think about the 13 seconds which kept me from being covered in rubble after a 107mm round came down through the building when I was deployed to Afghanistan. *I survived.* I did not have an alternate plan while going through Survival School. I was one of two females in my career field who had ever gone through the training program. I did not have an alternate plan when I joined the military. *I just survived!* I grew up living around the world and graduating from a high school in which very few individuals looked like me. *I survived.* Not having an alternate option was the norm for me. Growing up, I did not see anyone who looked like me and did the same activities as me. *I survived.* Thank goodness I was adopted young by a military couple who did not focus on traditional gender roles. If I had not, I would have been a part of a lower caste system, becoming a factory worker or just surviving.

How I entered this world is how I am living my life. I foresee my life continuing along this route; *I am surviving.* Like a phoenix, I will always rise again. The bike is repaired, and I too, am soon to be repaired and back to the life of surviving on two-wheel adventures. If you see me on the road, just give me a wave and enjoy the *wind therapy!*

aka Java

Notes

_____

_____

_____

_____

_____

_____

_____

_____

_____

Author L Michelle Jewell

Author L Michelle Jewell

L Michelle Jewell, a native Washingtonian, was raised in Southern Maryland right outside of Washington, DC, and currently resides in Charlotte, North Carolina. TV and Radio have always been a passion, which led Lynnette to train in TV Production at CT 76 Television Station in Maryland and later Access 21 in Charlotte, North Carolina. Michelle received certificates for her training, which led to her hosting several shows of her own. Lynnette also has a Diploma in Computerized Business Systems from Computer Learning Systems.

L Michelle has a strong business sense and a background in sales, marketing, television production, and advertising. She has held the position of Director of Sales and Marketing for a local Maryland magazine and was the Director of Procurement for the Computer Ministry at her church.

L Michelle's diverse interest in politics, education, community involvement, entertainment, and self-empowerment allows for many rich, diversified focus points on her show. L Michelle has chaired different panels and workshops over the years and learned how to incorporate many different techniques from the best-of-the-best, over the years, to create her own unique and classy style for radio.

L Michelle's mission in life is to create a strong positive platform to make sure that everybody's voice can be heard. She is a positive role model who envisions herself as a motivational coach that will inspire others to learn that dreams can come true no matter what situation they have been through.

Regardless of who you are, L Michelle Jewell challenges you to understand that whatever decision you make; no matter what path you take...the road towards your purpose can only be driven by you, prayer and supplication! Only you can stop yourself from reaching your dreams.

I'm Still Standing

Every person has their reasons why they got into riding. My own love of motorcycles started at an early age, as I grew up watching many of my own family members on two wheels. Every rider knows and tends to get caught up in that melodic roar of a motorcycle's engine. Head-turning to see what was teasing your ears and soul with that distinctive deep and rhythmic growl as it makes its way past you. To a rider, there is something about the sight and sound of a bike. Growing up in Southern Maryland, all my family used to do was ride. The area back then was considered country so there were lots of places to ride bikes, dirt bikes, and motorcycles. Being able to fit in and do what the boys did was easy…especially since I was a tomboy.

As the years went by I enjoyed watching my family and friends ride on all types of custom bikes, sport bikes, and cruisers. I learned how to handle a bike early. I could ride almost anything by the time I was a teenager. As a young girl, I always dreamed that one day I would have my own bike. Motorcycling is an expensive hobby. If you don't have the resources to buy what you want, your dream bike often comes down to what you can afford. Back in early

2000, after years of riding on my family members' bikes, I was finally ready to get my own. I started looking around for a bike that I could afford that would handle the way I needed it to. My first bike was an older 96 Suzuki Katana. I loved that bike but everything that I had to do with that bike to get it together often had to be customized stuff. I learned quickly that biking was not only an expensive hobby, but that the bike you ride means nothing if you can't keep it up. Older bikes can be easy to maintain if you know the right people. Hats off to bikers who want to invest in brand new bikes; however, there are well-maintained older bikes on the set that will outperform some of the newer ones.

In 2005 I was introduced to the Southern Maryland bike community. Becoming a part of the Motorcycle Community allows you to network with people who are into the same hobby as you are…however, years ago, joining that community was not as welcoming or as easy as it is now. Having been around bikes all my life, I knew a lot; but from the inside of the community, the scene changed me in ways I could not have expected. I wanted more. I started networking and meeting more riders who would help me on my journey to riding. In the community everyone goes by a riding name. I got my riding name of CinnaBun from my cousin. Once I had my name from that moment on I set about building comradery. I had unique friendships, and welcomed the prestige of being respected on the set. In 2006 I officially entered into the community the right way... by learning the laws, learning the skills, and becoming officially endorsed to ride.

As I learned about the community I started to see the many different sides of it. As a female rider, I wanted to have a strong network of support. So I made a decision to prospect for a club. I was not a prospect long, as this family-run club taught me a whole lot of what I was not going to put up with. Sometimes you have to know more about what you want and need from people who you will be associated with. Many people join clubs just because they want to belong and often end up club hopping when the club turns out not to be a good fit for them. I didn't want that for myself. I started having visions of what type of club I wanted to be a part of, so I decided around the end of 06, early 07, to start my own club.

As a female who grew up riding around males, I knew I wanted my club to be co-ed, having both male and female riders. I called my club, Beltway Ryderz. I was the founder and president, but what I didn't realize until I really got into it, was that there was something powerful about being in charge. I'm not going to say that the power did not change me in some ways. I quickly experienced the satisfying feeling of being on top of the world that comes with being respected in the community. While I embraced my position as president and founder of a club, I didn't realize the struggle and the problems I was going to have being a female president of a co-ed club, in a male-dominated community.

Even though there have been changes over the last decade, the reality is that the Motorcycle Community was and still is a male-dominant world. MC stands for many different things, but in the "bike" world, MC stands for Male Club or Men's Club. While there had long been female riders on the set, holding their own, at that time, I think ridership for women was less than 30% compared to 70% males. Over time, I witnessed women ridership increase. However, at the time, this was a male-dominated community and I encountered many problems getting my club started. Learning what I needed to know was not easy. I asked many questions. I wanted to know the dos and the don'ts. I eventually found some extremely great mentors who helped me get my program together. Still, I was having problems with a few people, including a particular that kept trying to bully me and trying to prevent me from getting my club together. While most men have no problem with women being on the set, I found that many of them were closed-minded and went out of their way to cause problems because I was a female in charge with an intimidating presence. Many females would have folded, but I was determined to stand my ground. I was 5'2", but I knew how to push and buck back at the people who sought to shut me down.

One thing about me, I'm not that easily persuaded or bullied. Coming on to the set with fresh ideas and thoughts, I was quick to make friends, hang out, mingle and get to see what the atmosphere was in the community. I was told to get to know everybody, and support everybody, and I did just that. Yet, people had a problem with that.

When I came on the set some of the clubs didn't have the proper paperwork, and didn't have any real structure. A lot of clubs were just popping up every other week as people thought they could just create a club without any rules, or regulations and make it work. While many of the clubs that were popping up had no rules and it worked for them, it would not for me. I always found out doing things in the proper order was the right thing to do, and a lot of people got upset at what I was attempting to do. When I set my mind on something, I keep going until I own it. Building my club would be no different.

I did my due diligence to start Beltway Ryderz. I did my research and figured out with the help of my friends and supporters everything I needed to do in order to build a solid foundation to get my club up and running. The first thing I had to make sure of was that my club could be recognized distinctively by our patch. My cousin set about designing a logo that I would use on our vest. Once my cousin designed the logo, I knew I had to protect my vision so I took the time to complete all the paperwork needed to get my club name and logo trademarked. I then developed applications, designed business cards, wrote bylaws, created brochures, and designed an entire package for prospective members with everything they needed to know about how to become a member of Beltway Ryderz. While I was doing everything I knew to develop, brand, and market my club the right way, some people in the community were starting to get mad at what I was doing. Facing opposition from a handful of people did not deter my vision. By this time, I had everything put together that I needed to start my club.

By the end of 07 my club was up and running secretly. There were many people talking down about me and my club and were actively interfering with my recruitment of new members; especially the male riders who wanted to join. As a female rider, I had started to earn respect in the community. However, as a female president of a co-ed motorcycle club, I was starting to be put into many situations that I had to fight my way through. The animosity some of the men in the community had towards me was not subtle at all. Some may have hid it in front of me, but many made it known. My presence as a President was not truly welcomed with open arms.

The reason why I chose the name, *Beltway Ryderz*, was because the Beltway where I lived in Maryland was a complete circle around the hub we call the DMV. The 495 loop known as the beltway went through Maryland and Virginia and surrounded all of DC. Just starting out, the trouble that I had, I don't wish on anybody. Creating a club is about building the foundation, a structure, friendships, trust, and safety for all your riders. If you don't have a solid foundation, dedicated and loyal people, the club won't last. While my vision for Beltway Ryderz was sound, my downfall was not having the right people supporting my vision. While I did everything I could to recruit people who I thought would be a good fit, I never planned for people who would come in with hidden agendas. Recruiting quality members is not easy. While I had some solid people on my team, reaping the vision I created at events and supporting other clubs, my vision was short-lived. It only took a few male members in a personal war against me, to turn my club upside down! It was a bitter pill to swallow as I watched everything I had built get taken apart and dismantled because a few men had an issue with a woman being in charge.

I know that I've been blessed to say I've been a part of the MC community. I also realize that the hurt and the pain of the personal attacks against me actually helped build and strengthen me. I wouldn't wish my experience on anybody. However, the flip side of it is, the challenges of being part of something bigger than you, will either make or break you. I'm a living, testimonial witness to making it! The things I encountered didn't break me; they made me even stronger. After taking a break from the set, I realized that every time I hear the distinctive growl as a bike passes me...that sound still excites me because I'm still standing!

aka CinnaBun

Notes

_____

_____

_____

_____

_____

_____

_____

_____

_____

Notes

_____

_____

_____

_____

_____

_____

_____

_____

_____

S L Walker, Ph.D.

S L Walker, Ph.D.

Dr. Shelly L Walker is a native of Pittsburgh, Pennsylvania, and is the youngest of a blended family of five boys and five girls. She is married with two sons. She was educated in the public schools of Pittsburgh, Pennsylvania, has a Bachelor's in Psychology, Minors in Political Science and Sociology from Troy State University, a Master's in Psychology with an emphasis in Marriage Family Therapy from Chapman University, and a Doctorate in Educational Psychology from Capella University. Her published thesis is entitled: *The Lived Experiences of Teachers as They Describe Their Values and Ethics Within the Educational School System.* Dr. Walker is the author of *Mental Thoughts: Life's Thoughtful Thoughts to Think About,* and co-author of *Her Story is My Story: Her Truth, My Healing.*

She is an active member in several community organizations that include the Order of the Eastern Stars, Daughters, an Auxiliary of the Ancient Egyptian Arabic Order Nobles Mystic Shrine, the Order of the Golden Circle, and Delta Sigma Theta Sorority, Inc.

Before getting married and following her husband's military service career, Dr. Walker began her professional career as a Sexual Assaults Counselor in Pittsburgh. She worked as a Counselor helping girls who had been physically and/or sexually abused. She also worked as an Instructional Aide for the School for the Blind.

Dr. Walker currently serves as a Transition Program Analyst. In addition, she is the CEO of *Theories of Life Counseling Services* where she serves as a Marriage and Family Therapist, providing counseling services, mentorship, motivational speaking to all ages, and is an advocate for Domestic Violence at *Fear2Freedom Alliance.*

Dr. Walker can be reached by email for purchase of books at: *phdwalkerls@gmail.com,* motivational speaking and counseling services: *walkernwalkerccs@theoriesoflife.org,* and domestic violence assistance: *fear2freedomealliance@gmail.com.*

When Down...Someone Always Goes for the Crown

J ust like many things that came to me at a young age, wanting to ride a motorcycle was one of them. Why and how; I do not know. There were many nights I dreamed of intensely speeding down the highway and days I wished I was doing exactly that. I envisioned myself as the "Baddest" biker chick! I often chuckled from laughing at myself. "Silly me," I thought. "How am I going to ride on a motorcycle?"

When I was young, my mother did not have a car. What my mother did have in abundance, was confidence in me. She knew that if I fancied something and wanted it bad enough, I would not quit until I obtained it. I cannot remember a time that my mother ever held me back from whatever I wanted to do. There were many days my mother waited to see what new scar I would acquire as a result of my determination. She would warn me about my choices, but she did not stop me. She would say that she would look up from her sewing machine and see me hauling tail up the stairs behind my brothers. All she could do was hold her breath and pray I would not fall back down the stairs. I never did though. I always kept up! She and I are both surprised that I am still alive after all of that. I remember when one of my older brothers took the brakes from my bike to put on his bike. I did not know he did that. Everyone was outside riding their bikes, and I had to also. So, I jumped on my bike and started pedaling to catch up. I was going too fast when I came upon a sharp turn. I started to brake, but I could not slow down. A car was coming and I had no brakes! There was nothing I could do. I held on tightly to the handlebars and braced for the crash. When I woke up, one of my sisters was crying and pouring cold water on my forehead. I had fallen and blacked out. A neighbor saw what happened, and he scooped me up before the car entered the turn. You would have thought that I would never want to get on a bike again. But not me. The baby sister. A tomboy. Whatever my brothers did, I did it, too. If I wanted to be with my brothers, I had to pick myself up and keep it moving. Endurance is something I learned to embody at an early age.

Although I was a tomboy, I envisioned having a smoking-hot, curvy body, wearing tight ripped jeans, a white fitted tank top, and the most stylish motorcycle boots ever to be seen. Those big bagel earrings, studded black wristbands, smoked mirrored sunglasses, and yep that would be me. Let me not forget about my long, shoulder-length hair! My hair would be long enough to whip around when I removed my helmet. Why do you ask? Because that is what I saw on TV. My vision was riding through the desert; needing gas and I would stop at an old rustic gas station. I'm tired. I'm thirsty. I'm sunburned. I AM stunning! All eyes are on me. They were not looking at me because they thought I was stunning. They were all gazing at me because I was riding through the desert with no protection from the sun. I found myself laughing again. That truly was a dream of a 13-year-old girl. Then I recalled falling off my bike and blacking out. That memory had me thinking. How was I going to make it on a motorcycle? I quickly shook that thought away. I went back to imagining my dream. I focused on how I would look in my tight jeans, sitting on my motorcycle. I allowed myself to continue to dream.

Several dreams came and went. But in one particular dream, I wanted a BMW motorcycle. Blue with seventeen-inch wheels, ragged black hard case saddlebags, and the BMW emblem displayed on the gas tank. Weaving through the countryside. I do not remember where I was going, but once again going super-fast and hugging those tight curves. I leaned hard into the turn, amazed that I did not fall off. Yes, looking cool on a BMW. Why a BMW you ask? I could not say for sure. Maybe because it was an expensive bike. Outside of the different looks, I knew nothing of motorcycles when I was young, but I knew that I wanted the freedom to be free. No doors. No windows. No roof. What better way to be free than on a motorcycle? Looking back, I am not sure if I exactly saw riding a motorcycle as a cool thing, but more as an *independence* thing. It required balance and will. It was invigorating, lighthearted, and an escape. Then I started seeing the world as it was, and not as I dreamed it to be. People who have to work hard are not often alone. That is how I saw riding a motorcycle. Alone time.

I did not set a particular timeframe to get a motorcycle, but as time moved on a motorcycle remained a want until I was older and married. Then, after nineteen years of marriage and shortly before my husband's retirement, he and I went to the Harley Davidson dealership. It was at the Harley Davidson dealership that I learned that a motorcycle is called a bike. Just like that. The sight of all the bikes reignited my interest in riding. I looked, touched, and then I spotted it. A midnight black V-Rod. I fell in love. I saw myself again as that badass biker chick. Not on a BMW this time, but a Harley. I was hyped! My husband and I were going to buy his and her bikes.

I was cheesing with a big Kool-Aid smile from ear to ear until my husband turned and said, "I want to buy a bike and help start up a club with a few of the brothers."

I said to him, "That sounds like an all-male club. What about me?"

He says, "It is. You can ride on the back of me." I laughed because in my mind that was not going to cut it. Riding on the back of his bike was not a part of my dream. If he was going to have an all-male club, I was going to have an all-female club. It was not going to be just any other all-female club, but an all-female club built on the female ancestors who were strong in principle and advocated for others. I was born of the *Most-High* and it was time for me to grace the throne. I felt good and a bit nervous. I always wanted to ride, but none of my dreams involved a motorcycle club. Let alone an all-female club. I am a loner. I have several friends, but only three close friends at a time. Only one of them knew how to ride a bike. It was going to be interesting and required some quick creative rethinking. Determined I was. While working on my doctoral degree, a full-time job, being a mother, a wife, and a member of several civic organizations, the fortitude to establish a motorcycle club was added to my plate of aspirations. In not reinventing the wheel, it made sense to combine the passion to want to ride a motorcycle with my enjoyment of community service. From that concept, the first all-female motorcycle club was founded on the principles of the Order of the Eastern Star and was the first to wear the O.E.S emblem on our vest. Every phase to rightfully stand-up club that governs itself was taken.

I knew little about the motorcycle community but was well experienced with organizational structure and business standards of operation. All at once, I had to learn about the motorcycle community in detail and build riding skills. No surprise. Like most women, life issues occurred. My body started to rebel against me. I had horrible cramps and lengthy menstrual cycles. No woman in her right mind would want to sit for long periods of time, nor try to throw her leg across a seat of a motorcycle dealing with that issue. That occurred for two years before it was highly suggested that I have a hysterectomy. That certainly limited my riding. While recovering under the doctor's care, a plot to have the changing of the guards was set in motion. Although I did not want to believe it, I should have known. Attitudes started changing and I was excluded from a lot of things. A misdial to my cellphone recorded a full conversation about me. I must pause because I so do love my Lord. God reveals things in some of the most compassionate ways. Although I was stunned to have heard how that person really felt about me, I saved the recording just in case I might need it. Here, things go down like dominos. What was plotted to be taken from me, strengthened me. A club was never in my dreams, but I remained poised and continued on. I had others counting on me. Staying committed, the Lord realigned some loyal SiStars. Delighted and appreciative, I did not notice that the Lord had provided a second blessing among the group of SiStars. One who was living life in pursuit of her dreams. The Lord placed on her heart to assist where and when she could. Little did I know that the deep share *SiStarhood* we forged would be cut short when the Lord called her home. I will forever be grateful and treasure her in my heart. Her stepping up and stepping in was the true spirit of admiration.

Realigned and trying not to fail according to the three strikes methodology, against my better judgment and the timing and coincidences, I thought we found two like-minded individuals and would be a good fit. But these were wishful thoughts. Yes, a good fit at masquerading and claiming to know everything. I ignored my better senses and it was not one of my best decisions. I am not a weak person by any means, but I admit that I have allowed people to push me beyond any sane person's tolerance level. I so wanted things to work out. It was a short matter of time before true intentions were revealed. There were mindsets that no one could comprehend and were inconceivable. I faced mindsets of finger-pointing, wannabees, socialites, title-seekers, desires for recognition, demands showing one-sided respect, whining-about-everything, liars, gossips, joy-killers, and those who took pleasure in others' misery. Followers of one another cannot think without others co-signing. The most disheartening betrayal was the hidden agendas, long resentments, and wishes of failure of others.

Moving with the ups and downs, good times and bad times, and approaching a decade of overcoming challenges, sure did stir up the Devil. A critical turning point in my family's life was the passing of my mother-in-law. Sometimes people in positions of leadership are not always given the same compassion and grace given to others. There was no time given for me to mourn. So many lies were being told. Words were said. Judgment was cast. I was tired and ready to give up. I did not care. But God provided level-headed individuals who stepped up and prevented me from making an irreversible decision that came from sheer exhaustion. Woe! I dodged one arrow but that arrow surprisingly revealed that people were being pitted against one another. While I was still in mourning, I was led to believe things were being worked out. By the time I realized what was happening, it was too late. There was no turning back from the underhanded damage that was done to fulfill a single person's own self-worth.

The loss of salvable relationships was only the beginning. The mounting levels of bitterness and envy in the air were so thick it could have been cut with a knife. There were too many erroneous sidebar conversations and seeded nit-picking to provoke arguments that bled over into the decade celebration. The whining, purposely not dressing in uniform, intentionally arriving late, not helping with setup or cleanup was the beginning of a showdown and a way of getting back. But that was to no avail. The celebration was successful only from the dedication of three, and so what was supposed to be a happy moment came and it went. Who would ever imagine that being a woman being raised by her brothers when she was younger would be used as a negative against her? Offhanded comments were attempted to make me feel ashamed and believe my interactions with others were cold and not sympathetic enough. To agree to disagree about the fabricated misplaced issues and excuses was not received by them. The continued badgering of issues was used to try to make me feel that I was the common denominator of everyone's problems, and undoubtedly exposed years of a friendship of necessity, envy, and a means to gain the favor of others.

Once again, I found myself in the prosecutor's seat. During the good, but the unanticipated quick sale of our house, my husband and I were without a home because our rental property had tenants and our sons had lived with roommates. We did not think our house would have sold so soon. When the buyers' offer came in, we were out of town. We had not started the search to look for another house. We thought we would have time. We returned home to pack up a four-bedroom house, three motorcycles, a riding lawn mower, and two 55-gallon fish tanks. I had to search for an available storage facility big enough to store our whole household. Literally, after cramming our items in storage, we had to try to secure temporary military lodging and look for a house to call home. The madness did not stop there. I started experiencing severe pain in my breast. I was hoping it was a pulled muscle from moving our furniture into the storage units, but my mammogram screening came back abnormal. I felt I was being served more than my share of stressors all at once. I felt I could not win for losing. I had no energy. I was being demanded to engage in rallying others to gain position and status, but I was not in the right frame of mind. Because I could not engage in what was requested of me, direct assaults on my character were deployed to tear me down; it seemed unbelievable. Not being able to participate in the drama was the Lord's way of protecting me. The false claims did not pan out. Relationships ended with a dreadful and inconceivable outcome.

As time went by, I later learned that all the manipulated conflict was an excuse for their many lapses in judgment and not wanting to be held accountable for their self-serving actions. In looking back, all the mayhem from the verbal assaults, lies, disrespect, and confrontation was the straw that broke the camel's back. I am no stranger to a fight, but once again the Lord provided a SiStar to assist. She was a saving grace. Preordained as a buffer. The anarchy was not my fight because two separate games were in play at the same time. Like poker and chess. With everything that was going on in my life, surprise skirmishes were the last thing that I needed, nor deserved. The poker game placed a bluff on the table. I did not take the bait. The chess game move set me in check. I, the Queen, had checkmated. The move and pain in my chest were stressful but in fact, were a blessing. The Lord's diversion helped me maintain my wits. When in the midst of darkness, the light will always shine through. When I was young and had bad nightmares, my mother told me to recite the Lord's Prayer. Always remember the Book of Job, she said. My mother had several thought-provoking sayings as I was growing up. Two that I found to be true are "What happens in the dark, comes out in the light" and "What is done on the devil's belly, comes out on his back. My mother taught me to choose humility over fame. To value safety, integrity, and accountability for self and others. Sound advice that keeps me grounded.

I will not always be to someone's liking. That is just fine by me. No matter what I do I'm damned if I do and damn if I don't to someone. I am appreciative that the Lord has enabled me to earn every mile I pounded and thankful for every challenge and blessing he granted me. He fortified me not to be shamed into other people's demands. I was committed to riding well before I could ride. I was committed to helping others well before I was O.E.S. More importantly, I still have vivid dreams, but now I choose to live them out. I am a professional and respectful woman who enjoys riding motorcycles. I ride. I ride fast. I wear tight ripped jeans and fitted white tank tops. I am that Kool Badass Biker Chick. Established in 2009. I am Heavy Throttle.

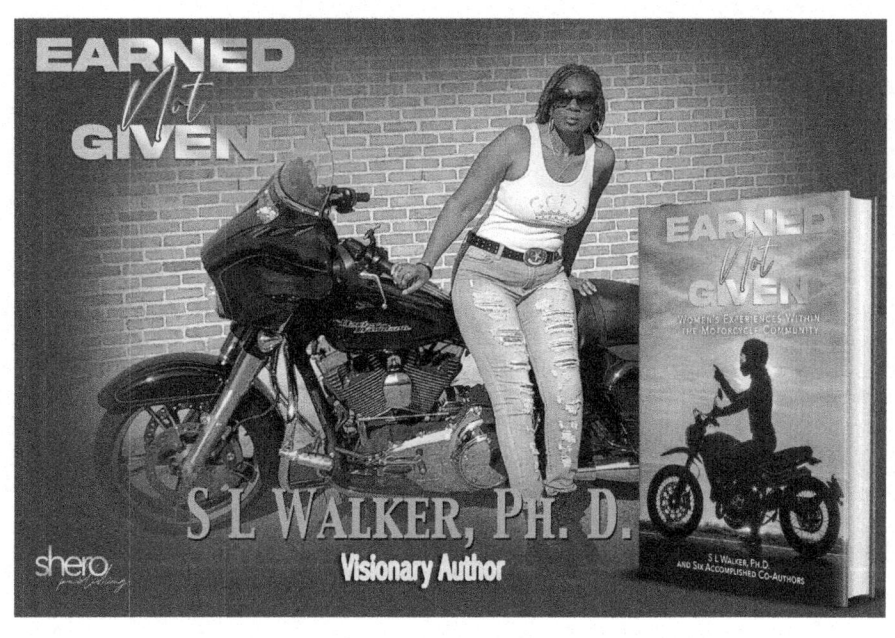

aka Heavy Throttle

Notes

_____

_____

_____

_____

_____

_____

_____

_____

Notes

_____

_____

_____

_____

_____

_____

_____

_____

_____

Notes

_____

_____

_____

_____

_____

_____

_____

_____

_____

Author Sheryl Gatheright

Author Sheryl Gatheright

Sheryl Gatheright, was born and raised in Cleveland, Ohio, and currently resides in the state of Maryland. Sheryl is married to her hometown best friend, David. Together they have four sons and enjoy spending time with their grandchildren.

Sheryl is a proud United States Air Force wife that traveled along with her husband, David while he served his country. During this time, Sheryl developed her own career path as a federal employee in Europe (Bitburg, Germany), and the United States Territory of Guam. While stationed at McChord Air Force Base, in Washington, Sheryl left the federal government and became a micro-business owner. Hers was the first childcare business to be dual-licensed with Washington state and the United States Air Force. This meant that she had to meet the requirements and pass monthly inspections for two agencies. As a parent of a child with Muscular Dystrophy, Sheryl focused her business on serving differently-abled children (children with disabilities) and shift-working parents. As a result, the United States Air Force awarded her for outstanding service to military families. At their final duty station (Andrews AFB Maryland), Sheryl decided to transfer her experience to a new federal agency.

With over 20 years of federal government experience, Sheryl is a Training Instructor, Facilitator, and a Certified Contracting Officer Representative, providing direct oversight for several multi-million dollar contracts and programs. In addition to her career, Sheryl enjoys spending time with her family, experiencing live music, traveling to historical sites, and embracing the culture of other communities.

Sheryl's parents migrated from the deep south during the civil rights era to the steel mill town of Cleveland, Ohio. She is the eldest of their two children. Sheryl has one brother whom she lovingly refers to as her "BIG" little brother. He is about one foot and several inches taller than his "LITTLE" big sister Sheryl. They both are fans of all things automotive and it was common for them to be seen on their bicycles pretending that they were motorcycles. After all, motorcycles were a big thing in the city and there was no shortage of motorcycle clubs represented in the community. Although her brother is younger, she followed his lead by trying to do everything he did. If he was learning how to ride a wheelie on his bicycle, so was she. If he was jumping ramps like the 1970s motorcycle legend, Evel Knievel, so was she. At Christmas time, she would try to convince him to ask for a popular 1980s toy, the Big Wheel, in hopes that she could ride it. Back then they didn't make Big Wheels for girls. In her opinion, her Brother was adventurous and had all the cool toys.

Contact Author Gatheright:
Email: slgright07@gmail.com
You can follow my journey on YouTube/Facebook/Instagram:
MrsShortyRock

It's Never Too Late to Ride

My interest in motorcycles developed in the early 1980's when the Honda MB5 was released. It was a black and gold one with mag rims that caught my eye. I asked my parents for one and my dad quickly informed me that **girls don't ride motorcycles.** I needed to know why and with every bit of confidence my Southern dad stated, "Because I said so".

Well, needless to say, that was not good enough for me. I found responses like that to be unacceptable. I made a vow to myself to remove the "no" factor from my life and I made a commitment to always work hard, do my own research and ensure that I would accomplish my goals. It wasn't until I became a parent that I understood why my dad tried to discourage me from having a motorcycle. Both of my parents were genuinely concerned for my safety.

Nothing is impossible

Then, as a wife and a mom, I would spend twenty-two years watching my husband and my brother riding motorcycles. I would watch them speeding down drag racing tracks and dream of the possibility of joining them one day. When they returned to the pits to relax, I would make them the best sandwiches. As they ate, they would talk about their track experiences in the most energetic tones. I would sit on the edge of my seat listening intently to absorb any informative nugget that I could retain. As they cooled down and waited for their next turn to race, I would ask them questions about how they launched off the starting line. They patiently explained all the technical skills of learning how to manage the clutch, the throttle, and anything else that would come to their minds. The one thing that stuck with me was when they said that the key to being a better rider was to practice the skill that you wanted to improve. I knew that one day I would fully understand this.

While I continued to focus on my family and my career, it became apparent that my sons were growing up, which meant they didn't need their mom as much. I was now thirty-eight years old, becoming restless and mildly bored. Clearly seeing my frustration, my husband asked me if I was still interested in learning how to ride a motorcycle. I quickly responded, "Of course I am!"

He promised that if I passed the motorcycle safety course that he would purchase my first motorcycle. Loving a challenge, I signed up at the local community college for the three-day motorcycle safety course, and I successfully earned my motorcycle endorsement in 2007. Feeling thrilled about my success, I made a whole event out of getting my endorsement on my driver's license. I got my hair done, applied my makeup just right, and picked out the perfect outfit for the picture. I was about to show the world that I was not only a Daughter, Sister, Wife, Mother, and Career Professional...I was also a BIKER. Now it was time for me to select my first bike. My Husband helped me to research several brands. I decided that based upon the type of riding that I was going to do, my best option was to purchase a 2007 cobalt blue Harley Davidson Softail Deluxe (The Rock). This motorcycle had everything that I needed to ride for long periods of time in the city and possibly across a state line or two.

I was so excited because this would be my first motorcycle. I can remember how proud I was when my husband and I went to the dealership to pick up my new baby. He rode it into the trailer, and brought it home for me. Some may ask if he knew how to ride, why he wouldn't just ride it home. Simple, he said, "Baby, this is your bike and you should put every mile on it." So, into the trailer it went.

We made it home, and my husband prepared to unload my bike. I watched in amazement as he backed that beautiful cobalt blue and chrome bike out of the trailer. In our driveway, he put the kickstand down on my bike and looked over at me with that handsome smile. Now here I was, standing in my reality as a biker and I became instantly terrified! This bike was BIG. I had made a huge commitment and I wasn't sure what I had gotten myself into. In seconds, several thoughts ran through my mind.

"What have I done! What, was I crazy or something! Who's riding this damn thing! Oh my goodness my husband is going to be upset when I tell him to take it back!" I was losing it, but I knew that I had to get it together.

At this moment, all I could hear was my Momma saying-

1. "I didn't raise any punk children."
2." If you commit to something, you better do it to the best of your abilities."
3." Piss or get off the pot!" Or her most famous line-
4. "We don't host pity parties here!"

I have heard these sayings all my life. After all, my Momma is the strongest woman I know. I could recall her saying, "If it's in my driveway I'm driving it!" In the 1970s, she was known for drag racing cars in the city streets and driving pickup trucks when women weren't known for doing either. Momma had no problem with rocking the boat and setting new standards for what women were capable of doing. She was authentically herself and I loved her for modeling this for me.

Reflecting on these moments, I knew that giving up was not an option. So you know what that meant…it was time for me to learn how to ride this Harley-Davidson! With my husband's guidance, I circled parking lots and rode around the neighborhood for a few months before advancing to riding on main roads with traffic. I dedicated several years to developing my basic riding skills. Before long I was crossing state lines, and riding for hours in various types of weather.

Follow the leader

In 2009, my husband asked me to join his co-ed motorcycle club, 'O'MENS MC Fort Washington, Maryland Chapter. Of course, loving a challenge, I said, "Yes." Knowing absolutely nothing about motorcycle clubs, I trusted him to educate me. He was the Chapter President, so what better person to do that. This education would prove to be more than I could have imagined. My first lesson was understanding that within the club, and on the motorcycle set, I was not his wife, Sheryl. I was his First Lady, and my name would be Shorty Rock, a full-patched motorcycle club member.

My husband had given me this name back in high school. Back then, he would describe me as the "Short girl that fears nothing and thinks that she is hard as a rock." From then on he called me Shorty Rock. The term First Lady established me on the motorcycle set as his lady. As the First Lady, I was protected by most of the men in the club and any male biker that had a high regard for my husband, aka the Club President. There were rules about how I presented myself on the set and how I engaged with specific members of other clubs. As the President, my husband had the final say on all things club-related. I even learned that I could not just simply go to the restroom without someone being with me. My club brothers made sure that someone was assigned to me while my President was handling club business.

This would sound insane to most women, but as a biker married to a leader within a motorcycle club, I understood. This life was very familiar to me as it paralleled my life as a military spouse. While serving his country, my husband informed me that I had to practice OPSEC. This basically meant that I had to be cautious about what I discussed, and with whom. He also stated that in an effort to protect our family while he was deployed, I had to maintain situational awareness at all times, and think and move strategically. This was especially true while living overseas. These skills were useful and easy for me to apply on the motorcycle set.

Now as I stated, there are rules on the motorcycle set, but we also had to establish the rules of engagement in our home. Club life could not consume our home life, and our home life would not be shared in public. In the house, we agreed to refer to each other by our club names if it was club-related, and by our government names if it was personal. People on the set knew that as individuals, we were married to someone. However, not many knew that we were married to each other. Eventually, we both would have to reveal that we were married to each other.

Apparently, there is nothing sexier than a man in a leadership role or seeing women riding a motorcycle. Who knew! I mean, of course I knew that it was cool, but I didn't think that riding a motorcycle was that big of a deal. I quickly found out that this life can certainly inspire some people to say the most offensive things to you. These types of interactions can tear some already broken relationships apart. Fortunately, my husband and I were able to maintain both an effective marital relationship and an effective biker relationship with minimal challenges. Respect, integrity, and trust will carry you through it all.

Keeping up with the guys

As Shorty Rock, I wanted to be more than a pretty face, I wanted to be a respected motorcycle rider. To accomplish that goal, I knew that all I needed to do was the following:

1. Mind my business. This would be accomplished by not involving myself in things that didn't add any value to my life.
2. Honor myself and my family by always presenting myself in a respectable manner.
3. Ride my motorcycle.

In 2010, I planned to build up enough endurance to ride the Rock six hours from Maryland to Cleveland, Ohio. I met my goal in 2011 when I arrived in Cleveland to the warm welcoming arms of my parents and my "BIG" little Brother. Seeing my family brought me to tears, I was so excited to see them, and they were so proud of me. Even my Southern Daddy called a few of his friends to tell them about his little girl that rode a big Harley Davidson motorcycle to see him! This trip inspired me to become a weekend warrior, making several short trips (less than eight hours) before eventually taking on my first long journey. I was planning a three-day ride from Maryland to Texas in 2012. We planned to ride ten to twelve hours a day in the summer, southern heat. I truly enjoyed this trip because I was able to see the application of my enhanced skills on the highway. Seeing other bikers on the road was also a huge motivator. I recall seeing one pack of motorcycles coming up from behind us in Arkansas and as they passed us I noticed they had one lady on a nice white Harley Davidson! She was the only woman that I saw the entire trip and I was so excited!

Rolling across I-40 was a hot and dirty ride, but pulling up to the event and hearing people shouting out my club name was the best feeling ever. We camped out, or as some would say we were "Glamping" because we were in our RV and not in tents. We spent a few days resting and fellowshipping with bikers from around the United States before gearing up to return to Maryland.

Adrenaline and poor judgment.

Adrenaline can help you get down the highway, but it can also lead you to poor judgment. It was on the trip home from Texas when I learned where my road limit was. We decided to shorten our return trip from three days to two days. It was our second day of riding and we were riding through the Shenandoah Mountains in Virginia, after midnight. Visibility was reduced and I could only see a small portion of the motorcycle tail light in front of me. On the side of the highway,

I could see the glowing eyes of the deer piercing through the fog. The fog put a strain on me mentally and I was exhausted. The roads were unsafe, and we couldn't see any exit signs in the distance.

Fortunately, we had a trail vehicle with us that was also pulling the RV. They pulled around us and told us to follow them. They decided to stop in a parking lot so that we could get some sleep. The next few hours were filled with the sweet sound of snoring from bug-covered, dusty bikers. As the sun rose, we were awakened by the wonderful smell of bacon and various breakfast items. We soon discovered that we had fallen asleep in a hotel parking lot which was next to a well-known breakfast restaurant! I bet the drivers of the trail vehicle knew that, but I certainly didn't. Yes, the FOG was that bad! They say that GOD protects babies and fools. All I can say is, "Thank goodness I am his child!"

When I returned home I found out that some of my club brothers and friends had a friendly wager that I would not complete one way to Texas, let alone ride the entire round trip. They never knew that I had my Momma's sayings and self-motivation that kept me going. I was determined that I was *riding this ride*, and I did. I had learned a lot since 2007, and I made note of the new things that I learned on this trip. Things like understanding the terrain of my travel route, and using reasonable judgment when departing. It was at this moment when I knew that I was bitten by the highway riding bug, and riding my motorcycle was the only cure!

Is it contagious?

My most memorable trip was in 2014, when four ladies and I planned a trip to attend Daytona Bike Week in Daytona Beach, Florida. None of us had ever taken a motorcycle trip without the guys, so this was a new adventure. We planned for months, discussing the route, gas and food stops, and hand signals. We purchased gear, tools, motor oil, sunscreen, and anything else that we could think of. Between the five of us, we had everything. We made the fourteen-hour journey to Daytona in one day and we enjoyed every second of the bike rally.

In 2015, I upgraded my motorcycle to a Superior Blue Harley Davidson Road Glide Special (Sweet Thang). Compared to the 2007 Softail Deluxe, this bike had much better features. Things like a better suspension, cruise control, GPS and a stereo made for a more comfortable highway ride. I rode this bike to several places like Key West, Florida, and California.

Is motorcycling the new corporate bonding activity?

Over the years, my skills were enhanced, which meant that I would ride my motorcycle everywhere. I would go get coffee, drop off my dry cleaning, or go to the grocery store for ice cream. I also enjoyed riding my motorcycle to the office. I never put much thought into it, but I quickly discovered that there weren't any women riding motorcycles to the office. I would pack up my business suit, heels, hair care products, a flat iron, place my makeup in my saddlebags and head out to the office. Upon my arrival, the security guards would validate my access to the building, followed by asking me to rev my throttle a few times. They wanted me to announce to the entire building that I have arrived in cubicle nation. And yes, you could hear the roar of my pipes throughout the entire building. They wouldn't let me in until I did so. It wasn't always this easy. The first time I arrived at the office on my motorcycle, security asked me to turn off my bike, remove my helmet and answer several questions. They even called my director to verify my responses. Yes, I had my identification which authorized my access to the building, but on that day it wasn't enough.

Many people would have been annoyed by this, but I knew that this was an unprecedented moment for the security guards and they needed to get this right. This moment made me proud and safe in my working environment. After my initial arrival, word got out and everyone knew that I was a Harley Davidson rider. As a matter of fact, my personal passion would now be included in my introduction by most of my colleagues, Division Directors, and Executive Leaders. "This is Mrs. Sheryl Gatheright and she rides a big Harley Davidson", followed by whatever they chose to say to make their point about my ability to produce favorable outcomes. As a result, I was invited by my colleagues to attend charity rides, other events or just simply to hang out. Little did I know that motorcycling would turn into the new corporate water cooler chit-chat. How could this rebellious activity be accepted by so many in corporate America, or as some people call it- cubicle nation. Small talk about the weather, and sharing pictures of our bikes would become the new norm for me. People who dreamed of riding were now obtaining their licenses and purchasing motorcycles. The office was abuzz with people talking about weekend rides, and customization projects. We would trade greetings that only motorcyclists understand, gestures such as fist bumps in meetings, and throwing the downward peace sign while passing in halls. I didn't have to learn golf to fit in, Motorcycle life was our new bonding activity. Since my arrival to the agency in 2006, I am still the only woman that rides a Harley Davidson to the office.

If I can do it, anyone can!

While balancing my career and enjoying life with my family, I was able to coordinate and participate in several community events. Over the years, causes such as domestic violence, women and children shelters, bringing awareness to motorcycle laws, and honoring historical icons moved me. However, it would be my participation in the annual Muscular Dystrophy Association Fundraiser, in memory of our youngest son that would remain closest to my heart. He departed this life at the age of eleven in 2009 from a rare form of muscular dystrophy.

With over fifteen years of experience, I am known across the United States as a Ground Pounder. I've enjoyed riding two Harley Davidsons, visited several African American historical sites, crossed over 26 state lines, and accomplished two Iron Butts. I was awarded twice by the 'O'MENS MC Fort Washington, Maryland Chapter for most miles ridden within a riding season, I was also acknowledged as a Ground Pounder by the 'O'MENS MC Dallas, Texas Chapter, and I was also awarded by the 'O'MENS MC National Officer Board for most miles ridden in a season. In 2018, Sweet Thang and I were even invited to appear in an episode of *Jay Leno's Garage* which honored the legacy of motorcycling icon Bessie Stringfield. In 2021, I launched a YouTube Channel, *Mrs. Shorty Rock,* which focuses on motorcycle gear, motorcycle safety, and how to prepare for your motorcycle journey. I also am proud to say that I made a lifetime of biker memories with some fantastic people.

Some would say that I'm a pretty good rider, but I would say that I'm still learning. Every ride presents a new experience, and if you are smart you will take the opportunity to learn the lessons as they present themselves. The first sign of losing respect for the bike is when you find yourself to be so good that you can't learn. Best believe that a bike will teach you who the boss is. I'll close out this story by saying the following:

If you are interested in riding, please know that it is never too late to learn how to ride a motorcycle. If you are currently a rider, may you remain inspired by the initial reason that made you want to ride a motorcycle. Either way, you should always remember that this is your journey, and no one else can ride those miles for you, but you.

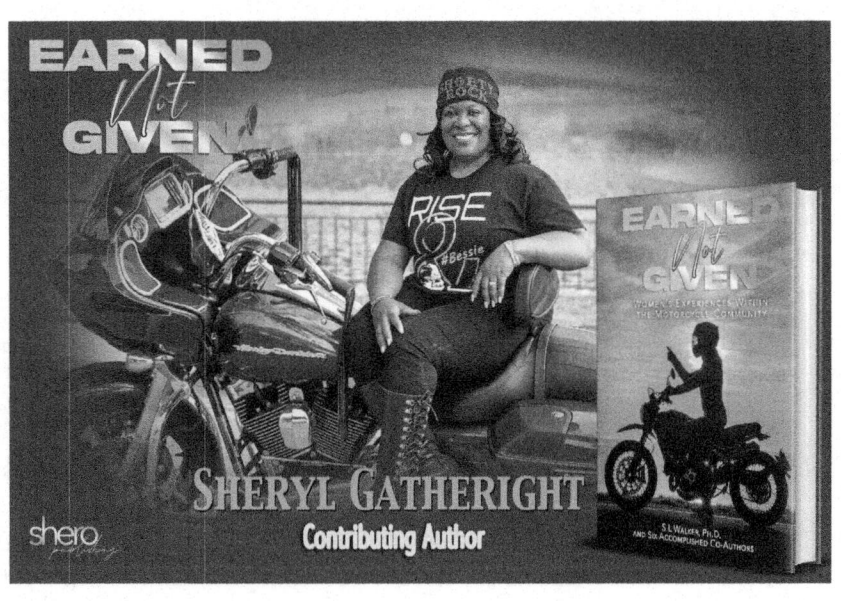

aka Shorty Rock

Notes

_____

_____

_____

_____

_____

_____

_____

_____

_____

_____

Author Star Garrett

Author Star Garrett

Star Garrett is a native of Soperton, Georgia, and currently resides in Killeen, Texas. She received a Bachelor's of Business Administration in Computer Information Systems from Savannah State University. Following graduation, she relocated to Jacksonville, Florida where she was employed in the logistics industry and completed her Master's of Business Administration with a concentration in Accounting from University of Phoenix. Star decided to leave the civilian sector and began her military career in June 2010 at Fort Sill, Oklahoma for Basic Combat Training and was commissioned in the Regular Army as a Transportation Officer through Officer Candidate School (OCS) at Fort Benning, Georgia. She is currently serving on her sixth duty assignment and has received numerous awards and decorations.

Star is a member of Order of the Eastern Star (OES) Prince Hall Affiliated (PHA), Golden Rule #66 in Virginia and Daughters: an auxiliary of the Ancient Egyptian Arabic Order Nobles Mystic Shrine, As Salam Court #214 in Korea.

In addition to her military assignment, Star is a licensed real estate agent in the state of Texas and a member of The Worth While Realty Group of Keller Williams Realty based in Round Rock, Texas. She is the owner of Flawless Smokes, LLC which specializes in custom cigar smoking accessories designed to enhance the smoking experience. Star is also a Scentsy Consultant, providing home and personal fragrances through innovative and customizable products.

Contact information:
Email: flawlesswrites@gmail.com
Email: star@worthwhilerealtors.com
Website: Star.WorthWhileRealtors.com
Email: flsmokes@gmail.com
Facebook: Flawless Smokes, LLC
Instagram: flawless_smokes_llc
Stargarrett.scentsy.us

Throttle TwiSTAR

My earliest motorcycle moment on record, is a photo of me on my dad's motorcycle, sometime around the age of four. He was the first man to put me on a motorcycle. There I was. A little girl with arms outstretched with my fingers wrapped around the handgrips. My legs were barely long enough for my feet to rest on the footpegs, but I sat there without a care in the world with a smile of satisfaction on my face. That truly marked the beginning of what was in store for me. Growing up I had pretty much owned every gas operated toy for kids, including a four wheeler, go kart, and moped. I always discovered new ways to be a daredevil on each of them. Even as a kid, I was always riding my own and was never that little girl to hop on the back even when I was with my older cousins. So I think that was confirmation that I would not be "backpack material" as an adult and would continue to be in control of my own destiny. Although I have a strong family history of riding to include both of my parents, I never imagined I would find my way back to the two-wheeled beast approximately 20 years later. It appears that my interest in riding was subconsciously instilled in me.

And then it began!

My journey took a sharp turn as I shifted from occasional rides, when the opportunity presented itself to being on the road almost every weekend of the month. I was all about work Monday through Friday and occasional weekends depending on how much time the Army demanded. In a perfect world, as soon as the weekend rolled around, my focus was getting some *wind therapy*.

As years passed on, I continued to ride but never really considered joining a club. I enjoyed riding on my own and attending specific events and functions at my own free will. No mandatory meetings, mandatory rides, participation requirements, and everything else that came with the club life.

While stationed in Louisiana, I crossed paths with a fellow female rider who lived in the area. We would hang out regularly and ride together on weekends and attend bike events. This place was the true definition of a military town. If you were out and about and noticed an unfamiliar biker on the road, the main mission was to find out who they were and what club they were affiliated with if they had a patch on their back. It didn't take long to link up with the local clubs and riders in the area as there wasn't much else happening in the small town of Leesville.

One day, I received a call from the one person I would always hit the streets within Louisiana. Our conversation started like any other but little did I know that it would lead to me being one of the first five to start the Louisiana Chapter of a particular all-female motorcycle club. During that time, I was undergoing some transitions that not many people around me were even aware of. Initially, I pondered on how smoothly this process would be and if we or if I really had what it took to successfully attain the goals and vision set before us. I am never really one to run from a challenge, so I agreed and everything took off from there. We had our five riders required to qualify as a chapter. The responsibilities and experiences that were intertwined with starting a new chapter were nothing short of a whirlwind of adventures. At that time there were already two other existing chapters of the Club.

Once we were established, I found myself balancing work, my personal life and the motorcycle world. It was very similar to life in the military; the hierarchy, organization, and structure of a motorcycle club were very similar. As a new chapter, we all had positions and responsibilities to fill. Otherwise, I would have been perfectly fine with just being a regular member who paid dues and attended monthly meetings. As a chapter, we were all at different stages of our riding journey and the experience levels varied vastly across the group. Some of the ladies were previously in another club so they had an understanding of common protocol and how a club should operate internally. Then there were others who had never experienced any aspects of the club life or the motorcycle set. Unlike being an independent rider, once you have that patch on your back, you are expected to follow protocol at functions and on the road. More importantly, you must know and understand the male-dominant environment in which you are operating. It was a constant uphill battle as we attempted to increase our knowledge base and increase membership within the chapter. At some point in the process, you have to recognize and understand when compliance outweighs commitment.

Over the years, I moved on average every eighteen to twenty-four months due to military obligations but I remained a member of the club. With every stateside relocation, I was fortunate enough to be within two to three hours of a chapter and/or some familiar bikers. I would always exercise my due diligence and participate in charity events and bike functions to remain active in the area. After completing an overseas assignment and being away from everyone for a year, I returned stateside and the chapter I helped start dissolved shortly thereafter and so did the club's bank account. I'm sure there was something in writing that detailed how funds from the bank account should be handled in the case that a chapter disbanded. From what I was told, it was obvious that club funds weren't handled properly and apparently were dispersed amongst specific individuals. I never bothered to inquire about how or why matters were handled in that specific way. My financial thought process was… maybe they needed it more. This was yet another perfect example of why you should only trust others with things you are not in dire need of or won't miss if mishandled. So after three years, the Monroe chapter no longer existed and I was the only member left standing from the chapter.

I kept doing what I had always done and never missed a beat when it came to riding. I was always viewed as the member who did her own thing. When it came to riding, I never relied on others to hit the highway with me. As time passed, it became more common for those in my circle to ask, when I was arriving versus who I was riding with. Most of the time I was riding solo due to the fact that I was not co-located with a chapter. I never had any issues maintaining my independence and I was always confident on the road. There were countless rides when I was the only female in formation. It wasn't something that I sought after but I would either get an invite or it was an implied task that I would be making the trip with the group. Sometimes these rides were as simple as a turn-and-burn for a cheesesteak run up the east coast. Other times it would be a ride halfway across the country. I was never the weak link so riding with the guys was never challenging or intimidating to me. I rode as hard if not harder than most of the men anyway. As expected, my actions generated questions, concerns, insecurities, and anything else you can think of especially from females who were predominantly on the sidelines. Due to their lack of riding, they could be viewed as local fair-weather riders or better yet categorized as just groupies with bikes. It's unbelievable how the most minute acts can cause you to be viewed as a threat. As I continued to ride and set the tone with my presence, I am positive there were plenty of conversations ABOUT me but never TO me. But was it my fault if you are known for having loose lips (pun intended) on the set. Yes, I said it! Of course, these side conversations are common and come with the territory when you carry yourself differently, so I never lost any sleep behind any of it. The way my brain ticks, my thought process was always, "if you actually ride more to demonstrate your ability, maybe you will start to receive the invites as well" There would be less time and energy exerted towards all the miles I'm getting on the highway. So yes, I have more miles and road trips outside of the club, but that's just how the cards were dealt for me.

Respect. It can mean many things on many levels. More times than not, it starts with the person staring back at you in the mirror. The level of respect, or the lack thereof, is easily based on how you treat people, how people treat you, or simply how people view you based on your intentions and actions. I tend to be pretty observant so it doesn't take long to notice that there are a lot of people both male and female who use the motorcycle set for their own hidden agendas. Some are there to chase sex, seek validation, search for somewhere to belong and feel accepted. The biggest mistake women tend to make is thinking they can do everything a man does in the same manner and still be viewed as a lady. Eventually, it becomes evident that you cannot expect to be taken seriously as a female biker when you constantly seek attention and get passed around as a result. You never know who is watching and may start to think that is how a lady carries herself on the set.

Being a female rider, you will always have other females who are either interested in riding or fairly new to riding who will quiz you all the time. They would ask me if I enjoy being part of a club and what the advantages of club life are. For everyone, my response is the same: there are pros and cons to being affiliated with a club just like being a part of any other organization. Club life can be enjoyable on so many levels. Everyone is different and has different needs, expectations, and desires. Being affiliated with a club does afford you the opportunity to build relationships and bonds that have the potential of lasting a lifetime. Sometimes they grow stronger than those with blood relatives. These are individuals that you expect to have your best interest at heart. After all, being in a club should be about sharing your passion for riding, sharing stories, and making memories on the blacktop.

There are two things I have never allowed to define or validate me as a rider. One is being a member of a club and the other is holding an officer position. Some think holding a position validates them or affords them the right to act a particular way without recourse, or a combination of the two. Sometimes a gentle reminder is needed to bring them back to reality. It's hard to be a great, fearless leader when you have zero experience being in charge of anything or anyone. I never expect perfection from anyone, but I do expect greatness after years of experience. With any organization, don't ever think that as a leader you can be nasty with people and expect to be respected because of your title. Clubs don't simply sustain themselves. It requires hard work, dedication, and most of all consistency when you're dealing with different personalities and mindsets and trying to achieve common goals. You have to be cognizant of your value and acknowledge when your time comes to cut all ties if the club lifestyle is doing more damage than good.

Low morale within the club, and more importantly, the leadership itself, plays a major role in its success or failure. You can't preach about sisterhood but on the flip side have internal cliques and side conversations that you think no one notices or is even aware of. Unfortunately, these are the instances when the harsh reality sets in that not everyone around you is for you. At that point, as an individual, there is no need to be apologetic for shifting your priorities and making changes that are best suited for you. Do what is best for you and not owe an explanation to anyone. As you progress in life, sometimes you naturally shed people, things, and relationships especially when there is no value-added.

Despite my constant moving, I will admit that I have established some awesome relationships and bonded with numerous female riders over the years. It speaks volumes when you see each other blossoming and making strides, and nothing but words of encouragement are exchanged, versus silent stares and hate. People show their true intentions unintentionally, so pay attention. But always be the best you that you can be and it will never go unnoticed. I will remain quiet and allow my odometer, road trips, and memories to build my resume for me. What will you be known for and remembered by? ...

aka Flawless

Notes

_____

_____

_____

_____

_____

_____

_____

_____

_____

_____

EARNED *Not* GIVEN

EARNED *Not* GIVEN

WOMEN'S EXPERIENCES WITHIN
THE MOTORCYCLE COMMUNITY

S L WALKER, Ph.D.
AND SIX ACCOMPLISHED CO-AUTHORS

shero
publishing

Made in United States
North Haven, CT
03 June 2022

19835031R00065